1

2

4

CALIFORNIA FROM THE AIR
TIMESCAPES

"Take heed that your flight does not carry you beyond that which is essential, but closer to it."
— Carl Sonnenschein

PHOTOGRAPHS AND TEXT BY BARRIE ROKEACH

WESTCLIFFE PUBLISHERS, INC. ENGLEWOOD, COLORADO

CONTENTS

International Standard Book Number: ISBN 0-942394-87-9
Library of Congress Catalogue Card Number: 88-51245
Copyright, Photographs and Text: Barrie Rokeach, 1989.
   All rights reserved.
Editor: John Fielder
Assistant Editor: Margaret Terrell Morse
Production Manager: Mary Jo Lawrence
Typographers: Richard M. Kohen, Dianne J. Borneman
Printed in Singapore by Tien Wah Press, Ltd.
Published by Westcliffe Publishers, Inc.
   2650 South Zuni Street
   Englewood, Colorado 80110

Westcliffe Publishers and Barrie Rokeach wish to express their gratitude to the Professional Photography Division of Eastman Kodak Company and to John Altberg, director of Worldwide Instructional Operations for Kodak, for their generous contribution of film and processing. All the images in this book were produced on Kodachrome Professional Film.

Bibliography

Austin, Mary. *The Land of Little Rain*. Albuquerque: University of New Mexico Press, 1974.

Engberg, Robert, ed. *John Muir Summering in the Sierra*. New York: Penguin Books, 1985. Reprinted by permission.

Hutton, James. *Theory of the Earth*, as quoted in *Time's Arrow Time's Cycle* by Stephen Jay Gould. Cambridge: Harvard University Press, 1987.

Jeffers, Robinson. *The Selected Poetry of Robinson Jeffers*. Copyright 1938 and renewed 1966 by Donnan Jeffers and Garth Jeffers. Reprinted by permission of Random House, Inc.

Lavender, David. *California, A Bicentennial History*. New York: W.W. Norton & Company, Inc., 1976. Reprinted by permission.

Lopez, Barry. *Arctic Dreams*. New York: Bantam Books, 1987. Reprinted by permission.

Muir, John. *The Mountains of California*. New York: Penguin Books, 1985.

Powell, John Wesley. *The Exploration of the Colorado River and its Canyons*. New York: Dover Publications, Inc., 1961. Reprinted by permission.

Sonnenschein, Carl. *Flight*. New York: Hill and Wang, 1963.

First Frontispiece: *Scalloped cliffs near Pescadero take on a salmon glow, complementing in both color and shape the waters that carved them.*

Second Frontispiece: *Mount San Gorgonio flushes in the cold, raw air above 11,000 feet. In the distance is Mount San Antonio, another of the peaks surrounding the Los Angeles Basin.*

Third Frontispiece: *Shadows delineate terraced vineyards on the eastern hills of the Napa Valley.*

Title Page: *Corrugated granite shields an ice-rimmed glacier lake — a tarn — in the high reaches of Sequoia National Park near Mount Whitney.*

Right: *Fermenting above the hills near Pyramid Lake, these clouds imply turbulence and rain below.*

FOREWORD

As a boy growing up in the hills of Santa Clara County, I loved the outdoors. I hiked in the forests of the Sierra and looked for hawks and lupine and salamanders in the streams of springtime. For me, the outdoors was a series of experiences — occasionally glimpsing a sea lion at Point Lobos, coming on a deer on Black Mountain above our home, confronting the bears that still inhabited Yosemite Valley.

As a child I took the environment pretty much for granted. Being outdoors meant not being indoors. It meant the physical exhilaration of running in sunny fields, of swimming in a cold mountain lake, of challenging the surf at Santa Cruz. Being outdoors was fun, and like most young children I didn't think of much beyond the pleasures it brought me.

With the passage of years into adulthood,

In the frigid hours before dawn, clouds congeal out of clear, thin air around Mount Shasta.

I grew to understand that the glories of California's terrain transcend the vanity of youthful self-gratifications. I came to know that California's coastal cliffs, high country of the Sierra and endless deserts were more than just fun; they were beautiful. Hiking along the John Muir Trail came to involve more than physical exhilaration for me; the grandeur around me evoked a profound spiritual exhilaration. Thus as a young man, I became an environmentalist dedicated to doing all I could to protect the highlights of spectacular California.

Although I did not know it then, I still had a lot to learn about environmental values.

Less than three weeks after I first took the oath as a U.S. senator, Platform A in the Santa Barbara Channel ruptured in the monumental oil spill that gave political birth to the environmental movement. The first bill I introduced in the U.S. Senate was to ban oil drilling in the Santa Barbara Channel for environmental reasons. Key among my Senate activities has been and continues to be the quest for federal policies that protect and preserve our environment and that promote environmental sanity.

In the process, I have learned a great deal more about the environment.

In the aftermath of the Santa Barbara disaster, I explored the largest of the Channel Islands, Santa Cruz. While unique in some respects, Santa Cruz Island is not dissimilar from the Santa Monica Mountains — hardly displaying the spectacular picture-postcard quality of a Yosemite Valley. Yet as I walked the dirt paths of this almost totally unde-

veloped island, I knew the importance of preserving it and began to formulate the legislation that eventually created Channel Islands National Park, including Santa Cruz Island.

What I have learned over the years is that the wonder of the environment isn't just the snowcapped peak at the end of the journey, but that it is there in every ecosystem we pass through on the way. From the low, rolling peninsula hills, across the Coast Ranges to the San Joaquin Valley's irrigated desert, up into the foothills of scrub oak, climbing through the mixed conifer forests of the Sierra past timberline and out into the granite cirque of the high country, we pass through separate worlds unique unto themselves, each full of beauty and wonder but each different.

As a child I was bored with much of the

trip, impatient to get to where the fun began. As an adult I find each stage of the journey fascinating and different, each worth contemplation and understanding.

Unfortunately, all too many of our fellow citizens haven't learned to appreciate this diversity of environmental values. While they can marvel at Yosemite, they often view the foothills, the plains and the desert as arid and worthless, useless except to rattlesnakes and ground squirrels. Nor can they understand why environmentalists object to motorcycles or dune buggies having unlimited access to what seems to them to be nothing more than barren desolation. They believe anything man does to the land — farming, irrigating, subdividing, mining, even dumping toxic waste — is an improvement, since it adds value to land that they

view as otherwise worthless.

Obviously California's 27 million people need to use much of the state's resources to meet physical, social and economic needs.

But I believe we should also seek to preserve significant portions of all our various ecological and geological systems as they existed before the coming of western civilization. My reasons range from the altruistic — the protection of our heritage for future generations — to the selfish — the biological value to the human race of preserving genetic diversity.

Currently I have legislation pending before the Senate to preserve a substantial portion of the California desert in its pristine state. Predictably, the California forest wilderness I helped carve out several years ago incurred almost no public criticism. This contrasts with the opposition now being voiced about the creation of desert wilderness areas. While there are various explanations for this, including the failure of many Californians to comprehend how fragile the desert ecology is, clearly all too many Californians value the desert only as a source of visceral experience like an amusement park, and not for its aesthetic beauty, as one might experience in a museum.

The great value of Barrie Rokeach's work is his ability to highlight an aesthetic quality of a landscape that would escape all but the most discerning eyes. There's a magic his camera captured in Death Valley's Zabriskie Point that makes any verbal arguments for preserving the California desert unnecessary.

To see Barrie Rokeach's California is to understand the importance of its diversity.

I wish there were some way that every Californian — and particularly every California schoolchild — could see Rokeach's photographs of the state's geomorphic provinces. Everyone who has seen Mount Shasta expects beautiful pictures of it. But Rokeach's eye has found equal beauty in the Sausalito Hills, in the rolling green terrain of Contra Costa and in the Colorado River at sunset. This book provides a quick lesson in understanding one of the most important political — yet nonpartisan — issues of our age. To see it is to experience the beauty and the truth of the wonders of that piece of earth called California.

— ALAN CRANSTON
U.S. Senator, California

Runoff from the scant rains of Death Valley National Monument cuts deeply into hills near Furnace Creek.

11

12

PREFACE

For days I had been waiting for the fog to clear off the coast. Each afternoon it would push back from the landmass, leaving a slender corridor of crystal air a few miles wide along the coastline, while the remainder of the Los Angeles Basin would remain obscured in its typical summer haze and smog. But that narrow band of clear air wasn't sufficient to expose the gem of an island "26 miles across the sea."

On the third or fourth day the skies cleared more rapidly than before, heightening my expectations, and so I prepared for departure. With time on my hands until the arrival of late afternoon light, I carefully examined the airplane and my photo equipment, running through checklists memorized years before. These rote repetitions helped clear my mind of preconceptions so I would be open to the new experiences that lay before me.

The plane was parked at a small "uncon-

Abstract designs emerge from the indigo blue waters and marbled ice of Saddlebag Lake near Tioga Pass.

trolled" airport lying along the coast between the busy tarmacs of Long Beach and Orange County. With free spirits born of the unbound skies, planes come and go on their own, their pilots cooperating in harmony without outside direction. Spectators can sit on wooden benches on the grass, enjoying coffee as they watch the incoming pilots negotiate the too-short, too-narrow single runway in need of repair. There's not much margin for error — it measures your piloting skills just to land. As I finished my equipment check, I recalled my flying instructor taking me there for practice more than 20 years earlier, and my first feeble attempts at precision control.

By late afternoon the wind was blowing stiffly and straight down the runway. A strong, steady wind is a good omen for takeoff, but it would slow the journey to my destination off the coast, Santa Catalina Island.

At 2,125 feet above mean sea level, Santa Catalina is second highest among the few precious earthen oases along the California coastal waterways. Though in one way overshadowed by the neighboring land-based mountains rising nearly 11,000 feet (Santa Ana, Santa Rosa and San Jacinto), this island suggests an ancient complex network of submerged valleys and ridges formed by folding and faulting of the earth's crust. With slopes leading deep below the ocean waves, like the hidden segment of an iceberg, Santa Catalina towers above its neighboring underwater basin, San Nicolas, by 6,000 feet — more than one mile.

From deep within the earth, forces of motion and heat have acted over the flux of time to mold the California landscape into 11 geomorphic provinces — distinct regions classified by similar surface features and geologic history — resulting in the most varied geology of any state.

Like much of the rest of the state, the Peninsular Ranges Province in the southwest (encompassing Santa Catalina) has a convoluted and contorted history of mountain building: from long periods of sedimentary accumulation far below the ocean surface, to volcanism, folding, faulting and deformation through heat and pressure. But unlike in the other provinces, erosion has been the dominant force shaping the face of these ranges over the last 100 million years, giving them the rounded profile we know today.

The Peninsular Ranges Province, though distinct, embraces a representative variety of landscapes from across the various regions — coastal vistas and expansive deserts, high granite mountains and flat sedimentary basins, earthquake fault valleys and volcanic rocks. It is exemplary in another way as well: as the face of the land changes through time, so does our understanding of it. The marine region of the province, extending seaward as much as 30 miles, is now associated by some geologists with a 12th "offshore" province running the entire length of the state.

The air was clear and smooth for my brief flight across the expanse of ocean. Rounding the southwestern end of Santa Catalina, I came upon a near-vertical rock cliff dropping more than 1,000 feet into the turquoise

13

Pacific. This side of the island acts as a dramatic rampart to the softly undulating hills that slope toward the scant harbors and communities on the northeastern side facing Los Angeles. Rockslides and deep, vertical lines carved by erosion exaggerate the perpendicular facade, as do scattered plants clinging to its sparse soil.

A blanket of fog, nudged by the wind but held at bay by radiations from the warm earth, hovered a short distance seaward from the cliff. Here, as everywhere, the weather shapes the earth and is itself controlled by landforms. I circled and swooped low along the coastline, enjoying its subdued curve receding into a distance framed by icy cirrus clouds. With my lenses locked on infinity, I began to frame the land myself through the open rectangle of the window, hearing and feeling the changes in the airplane as we responded to the salt air.

Piled a thousand feet thick by eons of mountain runoff, blanched salt deposits in Death Valley National Monument take on the blue of the sky.

Engines purr sweetly on occasions like this, so I was able to fully concentrate my other senses on the scene before me. Adjusting the speed, position and bank of my craft more by instinct than by design, I strolled back and forth along the coastline.

Alternately concentrating and relaxing, I created images for this book, taking full advantage of the coalescing clouds, land, sun and clear air — air so clear I could see the mainland mountains more than 100 miles away. Here and there I photographed casually yet mindfully the valleys and ridges, sand and rock, water and air, arresting the flowing interplay of structure and content unfolding in the landscape before me. Yet I kept returning to that vertical rock facade, corrugated and reflecting orange in the sun's late glow.

As the sun sank lower, stark shadows fell sideways from the cliff's weathered rules — lines carved by erosion — and I noticed for the first time the matrix that was formed by these vertical cuts across the diagonal lines of formerly molten rock composing the cliff. This matrix of contrasts — of the gradual but incessant action of soft rain against seemingly impervious crystallized rock — was a metaphor for the geologic history of the province and the state. This is a history of landscapes synthesized through the slow evolution of time, revealing "timescapes" whose scenic beauty chronicles the invisible forces of creation and disintegration.

In the afterglow, as the sun descended below the horizon, I turned homeward, flying now over Pacific waters calmed by the motionless atmosphere, my mind racing. I seemed to be returning not only to the land-

mass, but back through time as well, retracing the numerous timescapes I had recently visited. My mind raced back 2,000 years to the genesis of the giant redwoods near Crescent City in the far north Coast Ranges Province. Back 4,000 years to the birth of the bristlecone pines 14,000 feet high in the White Mountains of the Basin Ranges Province. Back another 20,000 then 45,000, then 75,000 years over thrice-glaciated Yosemite Valley. Back two to three million years to an ancient massive lake formed during the Ice Age, now only a string of dry saline lakes in Surprise Valley. Back 50 million years to the first rupture along the San Andreas fault line on the Carrizo Plain. Back 500 million years to the oldest of all rocks in the Sierra Nevada, revealed by fossil fragments in the mountains near Lake Crowley.

It was dark now. The sky had traversed its range of colors, settling on cobalt blue/black. Before me was the runway, a dark strip surrounded by more darkness. I would have to feel my way down through the still night air without the benefit of runway lights.

The aircraft settled softly, but my mind continued to reel. Like the boundaries of countries distinguished by the spoken languages of the people, I had come to recognize the features and borders of geologic provinces by learning the languages of the earth. Yet, I knew that amid this diversity a common vocabulary emerges, words that speak of time stretching back dozens and hundreds of millions of years to create California.

— BARRIE ROKEACH

15

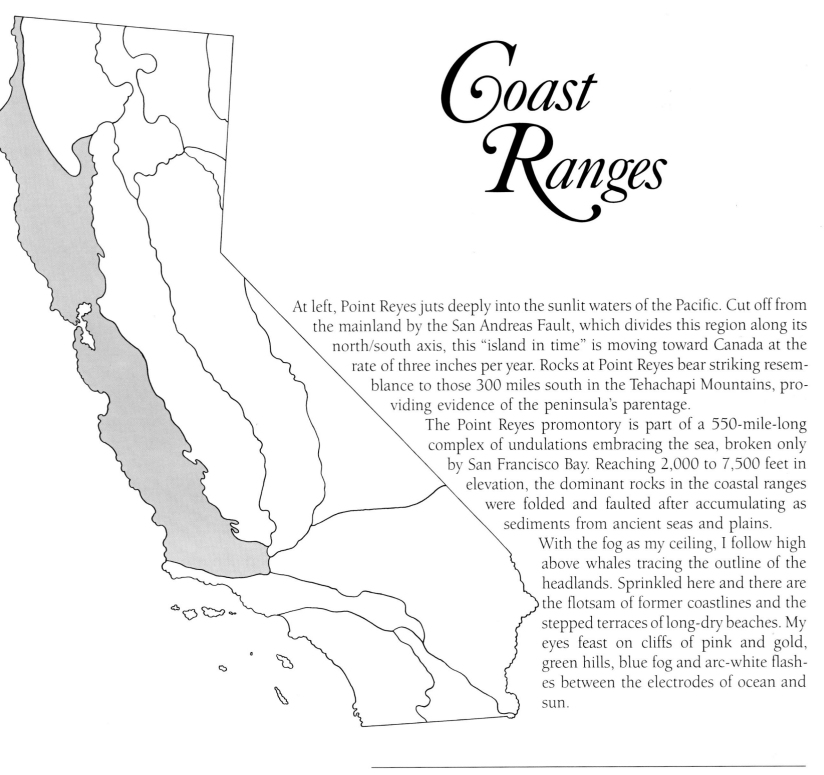

Coast Ranges

At left, Point Reyes juts deeply into the sunlit waters of the Pacific. Cut off from the mainland by the San Andreas Fault, which divides this region along its north/south axis, this "island in time" is moving toward Canada at the rate of three inches per year. Rocks at Point Reyes bear striking resemblance to those 300 miles south in the Tehachapi Mountains, providing evidence of the peninsula's parentage.

The Point Reyes promontory is part of a 550-mile-long complex of undulations embracing the sea, broken only by San Francisco Bay. Reaching 2,000 to 7,500 feet in elevation, the dominant rocks in the coastal ranges were folded and faulted after accumulating as sediments from ancient seas and plains.

With the fog as my ceiling, I follow high above whales tracing the outline of the headlands. Sprinkled here and there are the flotsam of former coastlines and the stepped terraces of long-dry beaches. My eyes feast on cliffs of pink and gold, green hills, blue fog and arc-white flashes between the electrodes of ocean and sun.

Overleaf: *The rains that over time helped smooth these Mount Diablo foothills now turn them into a sea of effervescent green.*

*An irrigated field northeast of Mount Diablo sits like icing
on top of layers of sedimentary rock that extend downward
more than 30,000 feet.*

*A low-pressure system over the Central Valley far to
the east acts as a magnet, drawing evening fog
through the hills near Sausalito.*

*"It is a good thing, therefore, to make short excursions now and then
to the bottom of the sea among dulse and coral, or up among the
clouds on mountain-tops, or in balloons, or even to creep like worms
into dark holes and caverns underground, not only to learn
something of what is going on in those out-of-the-way places, but to
see better what the sun sees on our return to common everyday
beauty."* — John Muir, *The Mountains of California*

*𝒯he ocean has cut through soft shale to reveal layers of time
embedded in the cliffs of Drakes Bay, Point Reyes National Seashore.*

*Waves take on the rhythm of the ocean floor at Santa Cruz (left)
and San Francisco (right).*

*Overleaf: Land and clouds merge into a single mass of flaming orange
in this overview of the Marin headlands.*

*"I gazing at the boundaries of granite and spray, the established
    sea-marks, felt behind me
Mountain and plain, the immense breadth of the continent, before
    me the mass and doubled stretch of water."*
— Robinson Jeffers, "Continent's End"

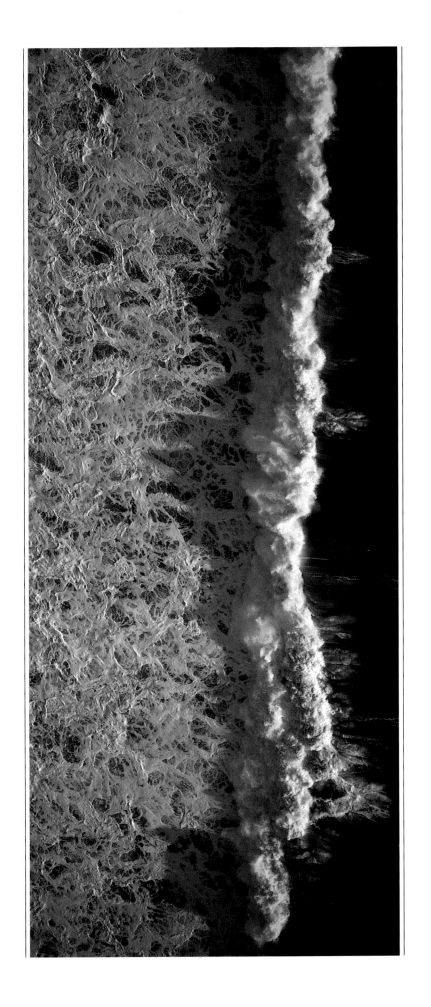

*D*ry alkali branches of Soda Lake in the Carrizo Plain take on an animal-like form.

Geometric designs of flowers in Lompoc (left) contrast with organic equations of vineyards on Mount Veeder in the Napa Valley (right).

"I did not dream the taste of wine could bind with granite,
Nor honey and milk please you; but sweetly
They mingle down the storm-worn cracks among the mosses . . ."
—— Robinson Jeffers, "To the Rock . . ."

At Redwood National Park near Crescent City, giant Sequoia sempervirens pierce a low-lying cloud to create a heavenly scene.

*"The stormy conditions of time and change are all abrogated, the
    essential
Violences of survival, pleasure,
Love, wrath and pain, and the curious desire of knowing, all
    perfectly suspended. . . .*

*In the morning, tule fog forms over marshland along the
Petaluma River.*

*Overleaf: Silhouetted against the reflected sun,
these marine stacks near Jenner stand as stark pillars
opposing Pacific wave erosion and representing
the coastline of eons past.*

*. . . In the cloudy light, in the timeless quietness,
    One explores deeper than the nerves or heart of nature, the womb
        or soul,
    To the bone, the careless white bone, the excellence."*
— Robinson Jeffers, "Gray Weather"

*€ucalyptus trees huddle against the morning dampness along
the rolling hills near Petaluma.*

*Only seagulls and an occasional hiker know the cascading
Alamere Falls at Point Reyes National Seashore.*

*"The earth was the world and man was its measure, but our minds
    have looked
Through the little mock-dome of heaven the telescope-slotted
    observatory eyeball, there space and multitude came in
And the earth is a particle of dust by a sand-grain sun, lost in a
    nameless cove of the shores of a continent."*

— Robinson Jeffers, "Margrave"

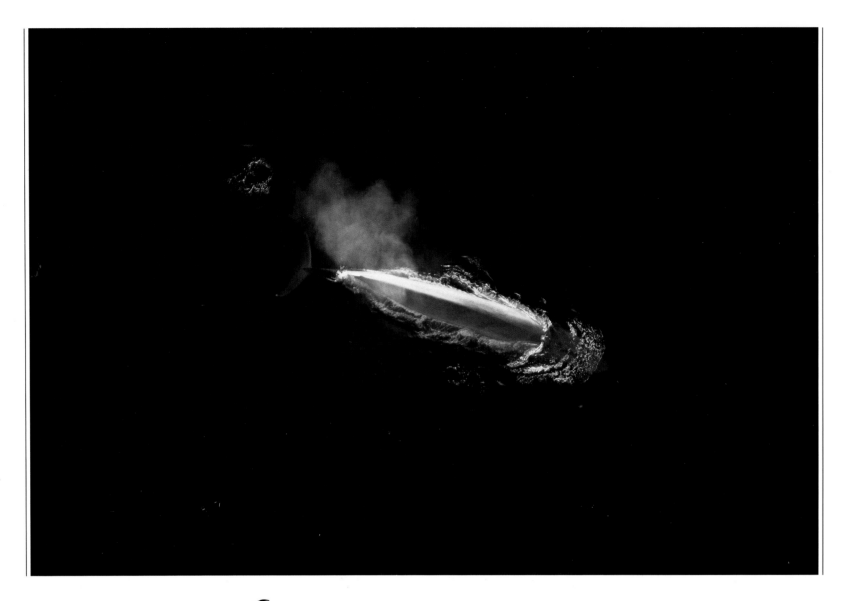

A blue whale courses through the protected waters of the
Farallon National Wildlife Refuge, a constellation of
stark islands lying at the edge of the continental shelf.

Patterns of drainage on mud flats at the mouth of Novato
Creek (top) parallel dozing elephant seals at Año Nuevo
State Reserve (bottom).

"The storm-dances of gulls, the barking game of seals,
Over and under the ocean . . .
Divinely superfluous beauty
Rules the games, presides over destinies, makes trees grow
And hills tower, waves fall."
— Robinson Jeffers, "Divinely Superfluous Beauty"

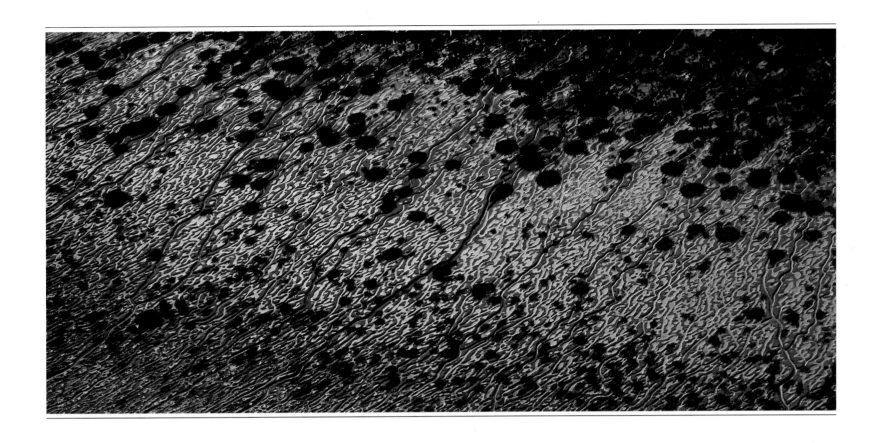

36

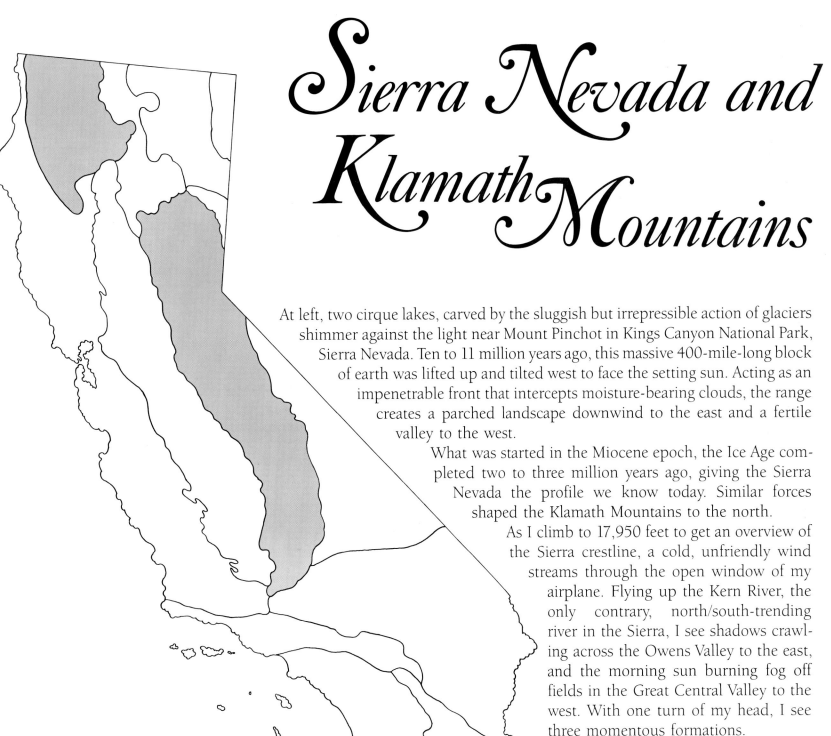

Sierra Nevada and Klamath Mountains

At left, two cirque lakes, carved by the sluggish but irrepressible action of glaciers shimmer against the light near Mount Pinchot in Kings Canyon National Park, Sierra Nevada. Ten to 11 million years ago, this massive 400-mile-long block of earth was lifted up and tilted west to face the setting sun. Acting as an impenetrable front that intercepts moisture-bearing clouds, the range creates a parched landscape downwind to the east and a fertile valley to the west.

What was started in the Miocene epoch, the Ice Age completed two to three million years ago, giving the Sierra Nevada the profile we know today. Similar forces shaped the Klamath Mountains to the north.

As I climb to 17,950 feet to get an overview of the Sierra crestline, a cold, unfriendly wind streams through the open window of my airplane. Flying up the Kern River, the only contrary, north/south-trending river in the Sierra, I see shadows crawling across the Owens Valley to the east, and the morning sun burning fog off fields in the Great Central Valley to the west. With one turn of my head, I see three momentous formations.

A few intrepid trees manage to find footing along the granite of
Boulder Peak, Marble Mountain Wilderness Area.

Dusk glows on snow-dusted peaks of Yosemite National Park.

Overleaf: *From Whitney Crest in Sequoia National Park, the crown of
the Sierra Nevada stretches far into the distance.*

"And after ten years spent in the heart of it, rejoicing and wondering,
bathing in its glorious floods of light, seeing the sunbursts of morning
among the icy peaks, the noonday radiance on the trees and rocks
and snow, [and] the flush of the alpenglow, . . . it still seems to me
above all others the Range of Light. . . ."
— John Muir, *The Mountains of California*

The Tuolumne River cuts a path through granite slabs downstream from Tuolumne Meadows, Yosemite National Park.

A small depression harbors water through the dry summer months on the slopes of Boulder Peak in the Marble Mountain Wilderness Area.

43

*W*hile it dominates the foreground of this view, Half Dome in
Yosemite National Park is actually dwarfed by distant peaks.

A serrated ridge arches along the Sierra Nevada in
Sequoia National Park (top), while to the north, Lake Tahoe
slumps in a fault cradle (bottom).

Overleaf: First light catches Mount Whitney in Sequoia National Park.

"Yet all that we call destruction is creating. . . . These Sierra
gardens and forests have been stormed upon for tens of thousands of
years, yet we see the upshot of all their long continued violence in
the tender and exquisite loveliness that fills them to-day."
— *John Muir Summering in the Sierra*

*T*he rocky spur of Thompson Peak in the Trinity Alps was
carved by forebears of the diminutive glaciers now resting
on its slopes.

Only shallow undulations remain to pool water in Desolation
Valley Primitive Area, a flat sheet of granite scoured, scraped
and molded by numerous glaciers.

" . . . during the glacial epoch, we would have found only fathomless
wastes of ice, with not one hint of the glorious landscapes that were
being sculptured in the silence and darkness beneath, nor of the
gardens and green meadows and glad sun-born pines. Yet the
glaciers were the implements of all this lavish predestined
beauty. . . ." — *John Muir Summering in the Sierra*

A line of aspen
displays fall colors
in the protective cover
of a shallow ravine west
of Bridgeport.

alf Dome, seen here close up and from the side, is a testament to the shearing power of glaciers.

Overleaf: In the chill, high altitudes of fall, the craggy skyline of the Hoover Wilderness Area near Buckeye Pass exudes a misty aura.

*T*wo views of the sovereign peak of the Sierra Nevada —
Mount Whitney on the eastern border of Sequoia
National Park — show the rough-hewn features of
the highest mountain in the lower 48.

"Here we caught our first fair view of the jagged,
storm-worn crest of Mount Whitney, [still] far above
and beyond, looming gray and ruin-like from a
multitude of shattered ridges and spires."

— *John Muir Summering in the Sierra*

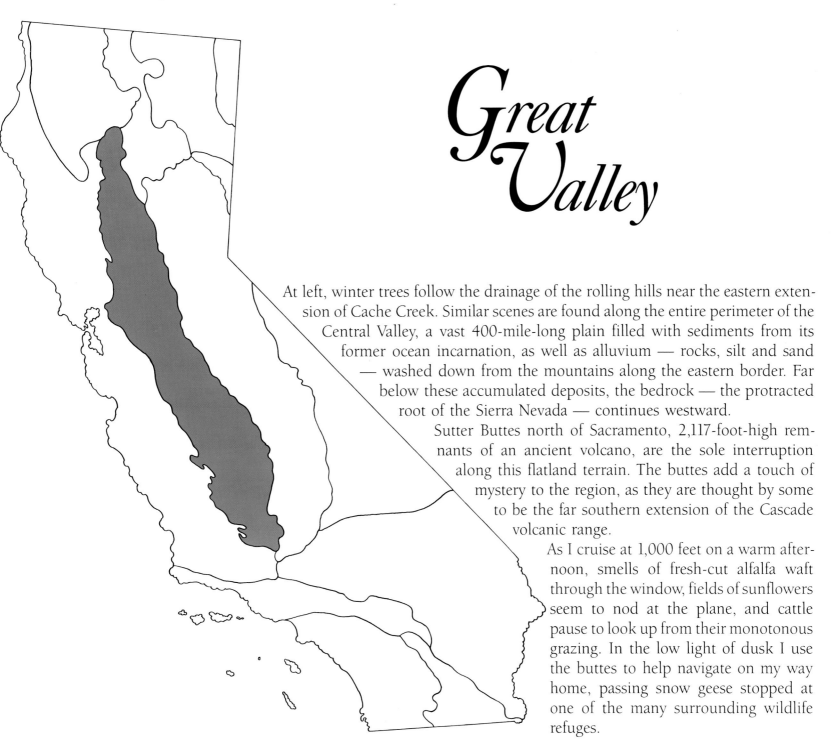

Great Valley

At left, winter trees follow the drainage of the rolling hills near the eastern extension of Cache Creek. Similar scenes are found along the entire perimeter of the Central Valley, a vast 400-mile-long plain filled with sediments from its former ocean incarnation, as well as alluvium — rocks, silt and sand — washed down from the mountains along the eastern border. Far below these accumulated deposits, the bedrock — the protracted root of the Sierra Nevada — continues westward.

Sutter Buttes north of Sacramento, 2,117-foot-high remnants of an ancient volcano, are the sole interruption along this flatland terrain. The buttes add a touch of mystery to the region, as they are thought by some to be the far southern extension of the Cascade volcanic range.

As I cruise at 1,000 feet on a warm afternoon, smells of fresh-cut alfalfa waft through the window, fields of sunflowers seem to nod at the plane, and cattle pause to look up from their monotonous grazing. In the low light of dusk I use the buttes to help navigate on my way home, passing snow geese stopped at one of the many surrounding wildlife refuges.

A flock of snow geese tests the winds northwest of Sutter
Buttes in the Delevan National Wildlife Refuge.

This tranquil almond farm near Winters suggests
the relatively stable geologic history of the region.

Overleaf: In a landscape already dissected by wind, rain and time,
Stony Creek leaves its own mark on the fringes of the Central Valley.
In the background rise the Yolla Bolly Mountains.

"Time, which measures every thing in our idea, and is
often deficient to our schemes, is to nature endless and
as nothing." — James Hutton, *Theory of the Earth*

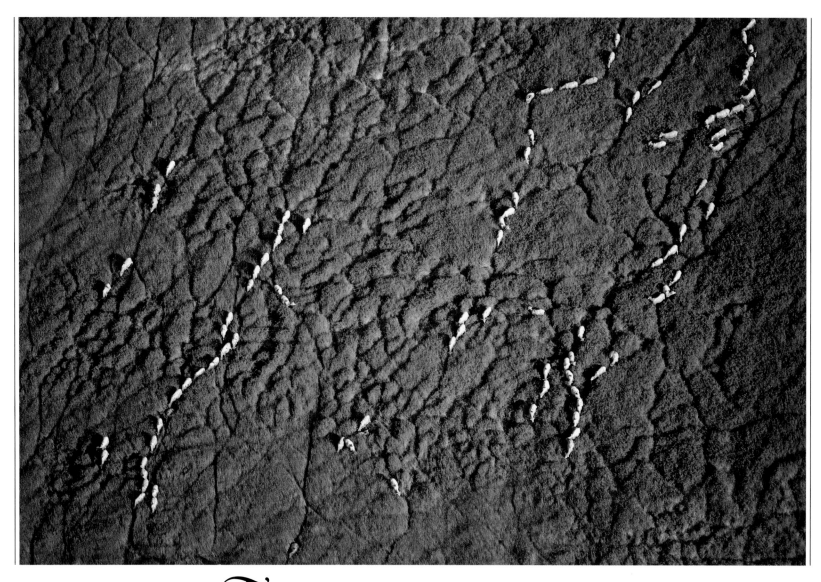

*T*races of man and animal are easily distinguished in
these two views of the Sacramento Valley.

"*Table-flat and deep-soiled, the vast Central Valley has no duplicate
in North America. The Sierra Nevada Range to the east draws
extravagant quantities of snow and rain from the storms of winter
and sends the moisture roaring toward the flatlands through
canyons from 2,000 to 5,000 feet deep.*"
— David Lavender, *California, A Bicentennial History*

*𝒜 sea of hills billows out from the Vaca Mountains
into the Great Valley.*

*Borrowed designs of ancient terrace flooding (top)
contrast with the architecture of western
ditch irrigation (bottom) near Sacramento.*

*"But nature's outstanding money-maker . . . is the deep alluvial soil
of the interior valleys, warmed by nine months of hothouse
temperatures. Once wheat . . . was the dominant crop. Now there is
fantastic diversity: rice, asparagus, sugar beets, hay, citrus,
avocados, grapes, raisins, dates, walnuts, almonds — a harvest of
almost two hundred different fruits and vegetables."*

— David Lavender, *California, A Bicentennial History*

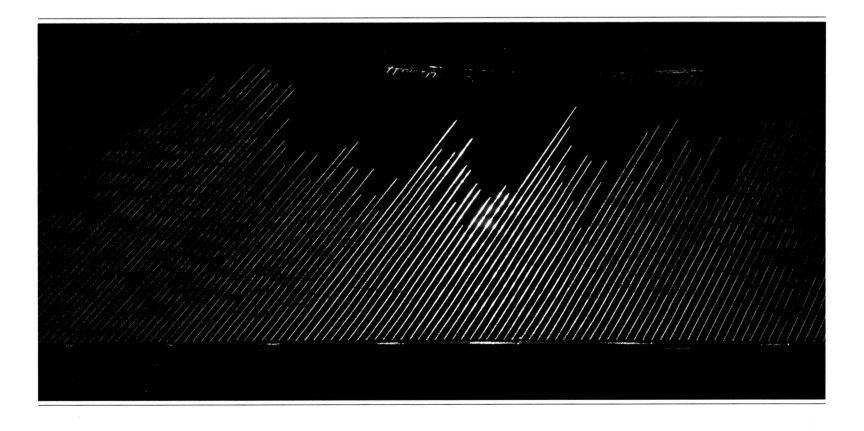

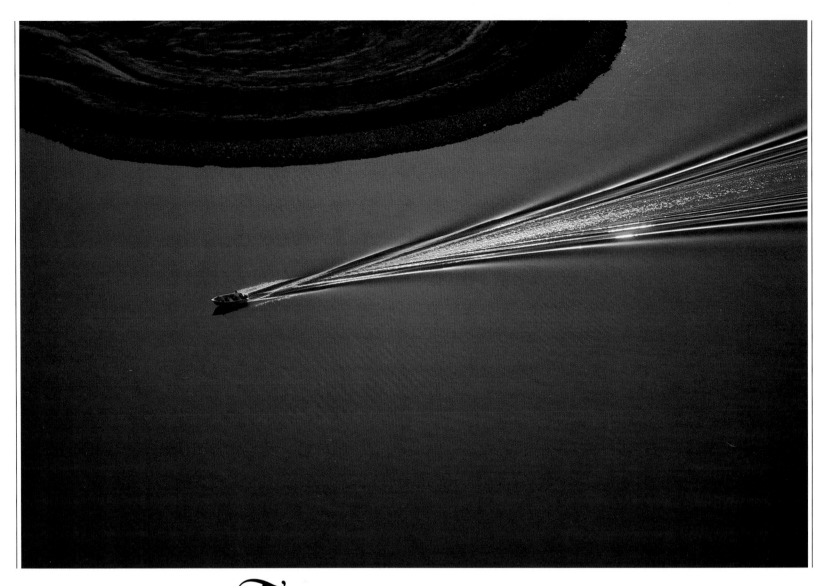

The Central Valley is the state's major catch basin for mountain runoff, providing an ample arena for watersports.

"Just before the south-flowing Sacramento and the north-flowing San Joaquin meet each other, they bend west. The area surrounding the confluence of their main channels is a . . .

*T*he Sacramento Delta drains mountain runoff
for rice farming and other
agricultural uses.

*. . . maze of waterways some 1,200 square miles in
extent known as the Delta. The Delta opens onto a
narrow strait that leads into the northern arm of San
Francisco Bay."*

— David Lavender, *California, A Bicentennial History*

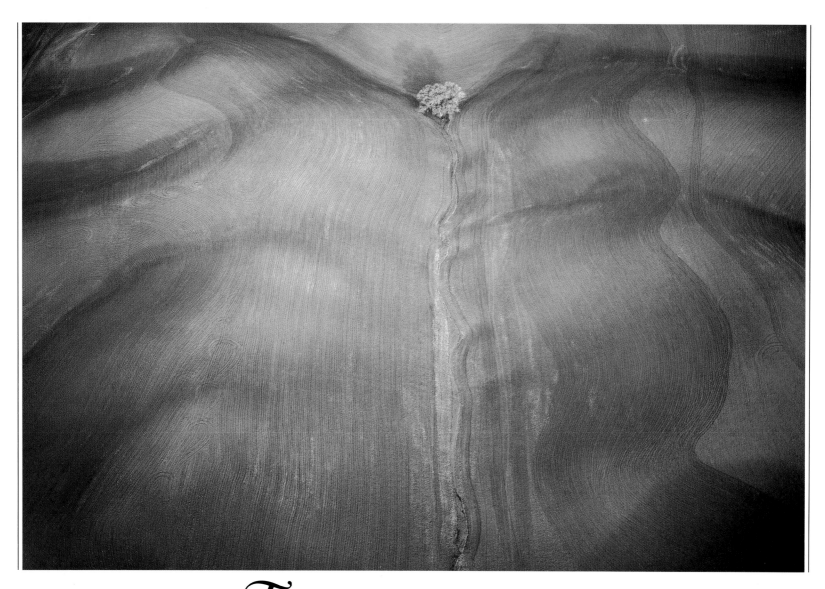

*T*he hills near Woodland have completely given
way to agriculture.

"*Some commentators have gone so far as to
call the state 'a window on the future.' If the metaphor
is valid, then it is well to look as judiciously as possible
through that window at some of the old futures that
are now past . . .*

*M*eanwhile, the Cache Valley resists the process
of cultivation.

*. . . and especially at California's regional
manifestations of the nation's unending dilemma: how
to reconcile impassioned drives for full economic,
social, and political freedom with the imperatives of
social responsibility."*

— David Lavender, *California, A Bicentennial History*

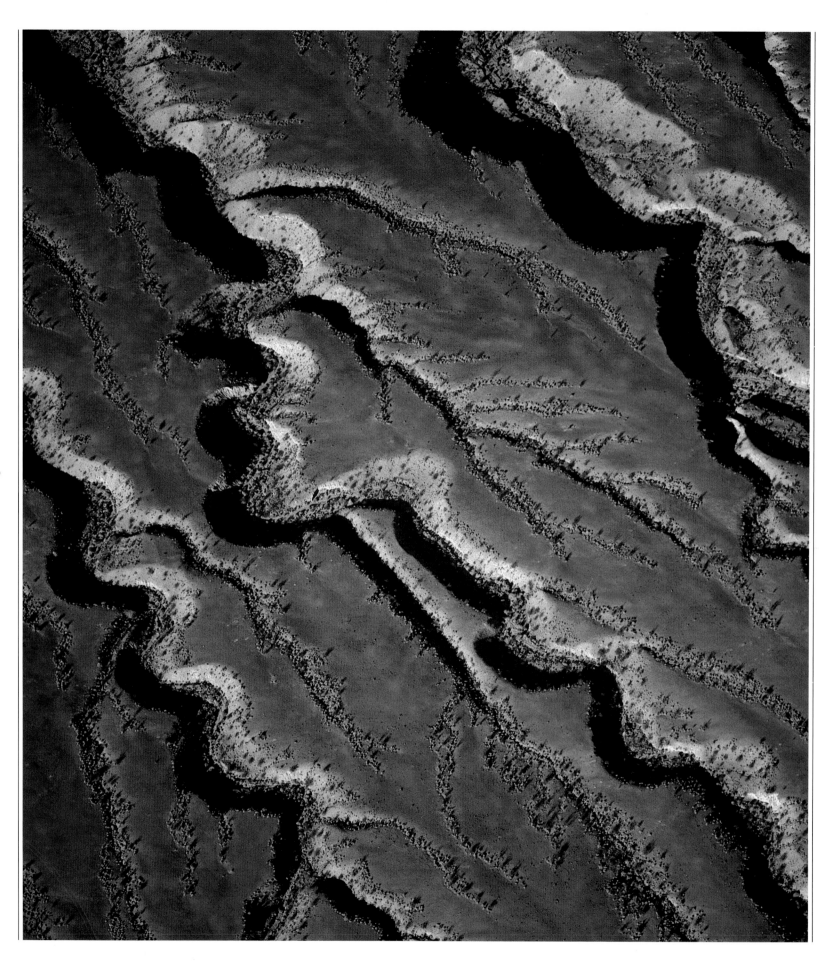

Basin Ranges

A landscape of extremes, Death Valley is the lowest (282 feet below sea level), hottest (134 degrees Fahrenheit) and one of the driest places in North America. It is also a source of illusions — dry salt flats impersonating blue waters, and sandy riverbeds wriggling like snakes on top of the desert floor. (Turn the facing page upside-down and the white squiggly ridges lying above the surrounding brown of the desert become furrows cutting into the ground.)

Death Valley is a basin surrounded by roughly parallel mountain ranges towering between 5,000 and 11,000 feet. It is typical of the many faultblocks — depressions in the earth bounded by faults — that make up this region and give it its name. A mecca in the winter, Death Valley is unbearable in the summer, which is just when I prefer to visit — I have the sand dunes all to myself.

You can find taller dunes in Eureka Valley, larger tracts near the Arizona/Mexico border and whiter sands in the New Mexico desert. But surely the most beautiful sand dunes in North America are located in California's Death Valley National Monument.

Overleaf: *Beyond Zabriskie Point in Death Valley National Monument, salt flats reflect the sky, giving the illusion of moisture.*

*T*he once-gushing
Owens River
saunters past Bishop.

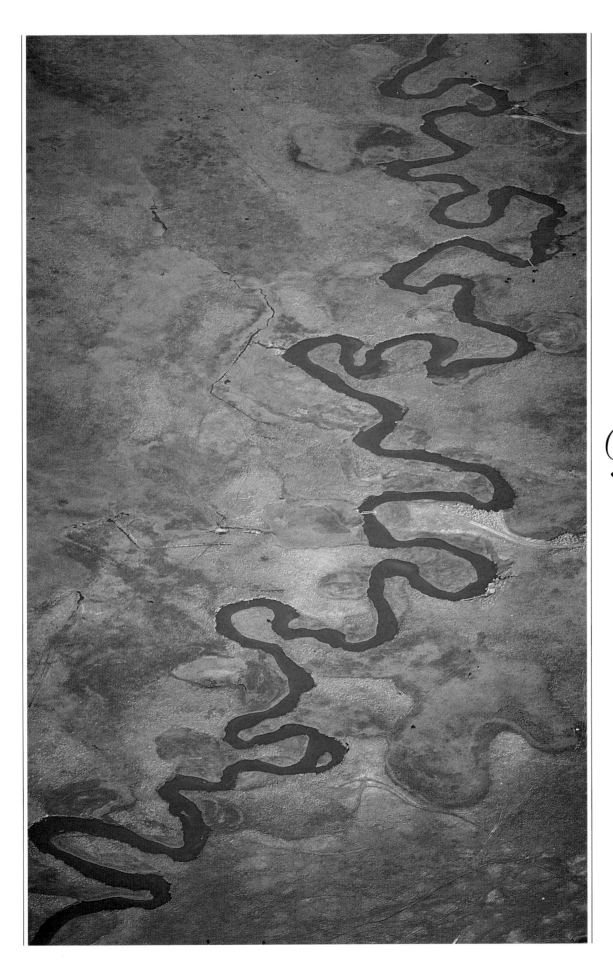

*arther upstream,
this vestige
of untrammeled days
winds its way
past Mammoth.*

*D*eath Valley National Monument is a shrine for sand dunes —
*ephemeral manifestations of the sculpting power of
the wind — including complex dunes (above), barchanoid dunes
(top right) and transverse dunes (bottom right).*

*"The earth is no wanton to give up all her best to every
comer, but keeps a sweet, separate intimacy for each."*
— Mary Austin, *The Land of Little Rain*

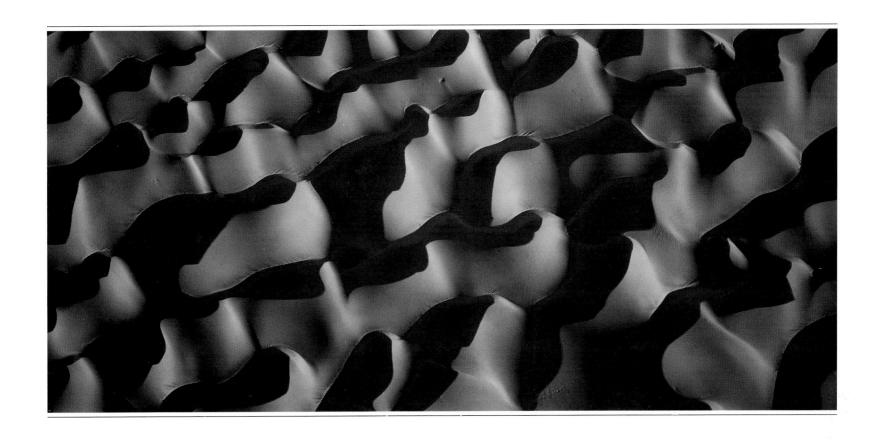

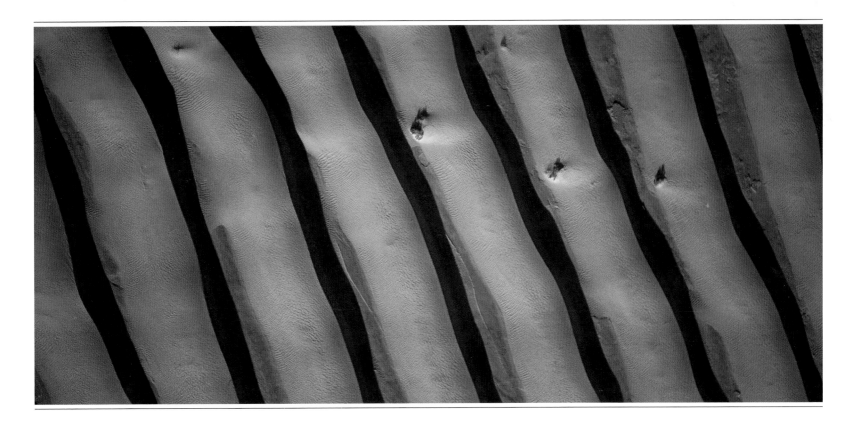

*B*eauty deceives here at Owens Lake, a dry alkali lake
bed that has been robbed of its vitality.

Fleeting winds brush across the surface of Mono Lake and
around its famous tufa towers, formations equally transient
and now exposed by the precipitous drop in the lake surface.

"After rains water accumulates in the hollows of small
closed valleys, and, evaporating, leaves hard dry levels
of pure desertness that get the local name of dry lakes.
Where the mountains are steep and the rains heavy,
the pool is never quite dry, but dark and bitter,
rimmed about with the efflorescence of alkaline
deposits." — Mary Austin, *The Land of Little Rain*

S̸ands and shadows of the Warner Range march across
Middle Alkali Lake in Surprise Valley
toward distant hills in Nevada.

Jeffrey pines flourish in the snowlike volcanic ash of
Mono Craters, a cluster of obsidian domes.

"In the broad wastes open to the wind the sand drifts in
hummocks about the stubby shrubs, and between them
the soil shows saline traces. The sculpture of the hills
here is more wind than water work, though the quick storms do
sometimes scar them past many a year's redeeming."
— Mary Austin, *The Land of Little Rain*

*T*he remnant of a much larger glacial lake, Mono Lake
wanes into a pallid abstraction along its shoreline.

Desert sands in Surprise Valley (top) are parched brethren to
the ornamental salts of Deep Springs Lake (bottom) at the
junction of the White and Inyo mountains.

"Here you have no rain when all the earth cries for it, or quick downpours
called cloud-bursts for violence. A land of lost rivers, with little in it
to love; yet a land that once visited must be come back to inevitably."
— Mary Austin, *The Land of Little Rain*

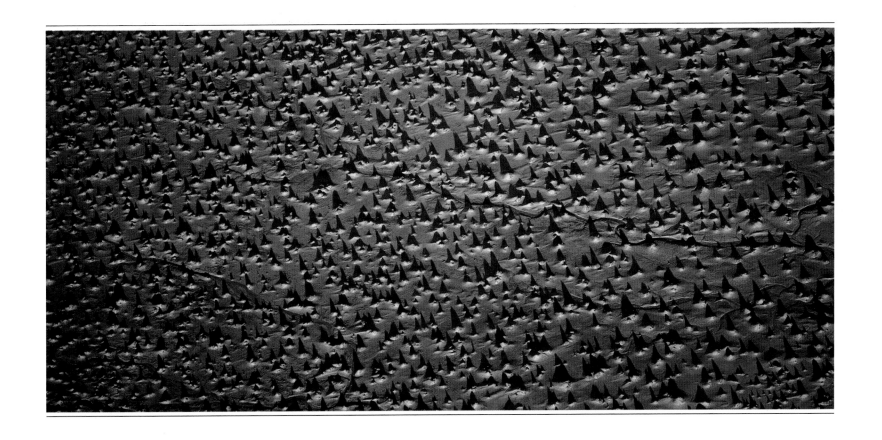

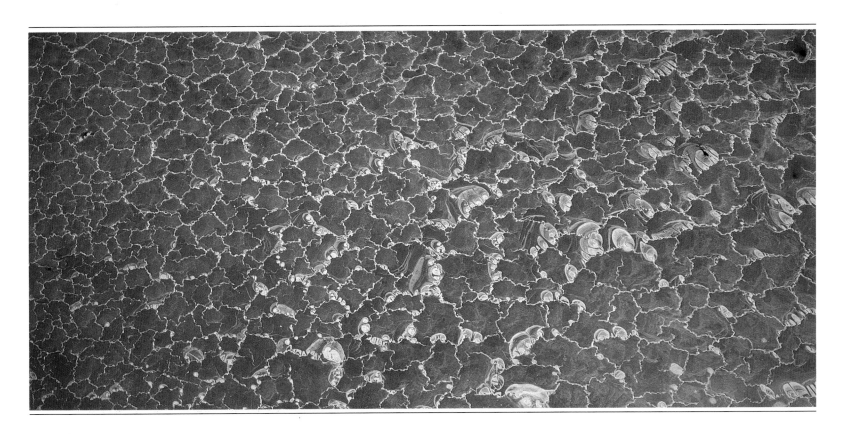

Cascade Range and Modoc Plateau

At left, the moon rises over the snow-streaked summit of the world's largest plug dome volcano, 10,457-foot-high Mount Lassen. Filled by magma — molten rock — welling up, it is the most southerly volcano in the Cascade Range, a region of fire extending through Oregon and Washington into Canada.

Similar in origin — and containing many small volcanic cones — the adjacent Modoc Plateau is a level tableland of accumulated rock born of molten rivers of lava and explosions. Strewn everywhere across these two regions are the colors and shapes of their violent creation.

Early morning and late afternoon are my favorite times to photograph: the light is low and three-dimensional in effect, rapidly changing the face of the landscape, while the atmosphere is often translucent, encouraging overviews. Yet just before sunrise, when the sky is still cobalt blue, and just after sunset, when the hand of the sun has left the ground — these are also precious moments. The land is at peace and permits introspection.

*D*usk illuminates Clear Lake (foreground) and Tule Lake
national wildlife refuges near the Oregon border.

Morning fog envelops the forest south of
Lassen Volcanic National Park.

Overleaf: Volcanic Mount Shasta casts daybreak shadows
on the atmosphere.

"The day was all sunshine, and the sun went down in a glow of that
delicious purple so common in sagebrush 'deserts.' But next morning
the wind blew stormily and the air was dark with snow-flowers."
— *John Muir Summering in the Sierra*

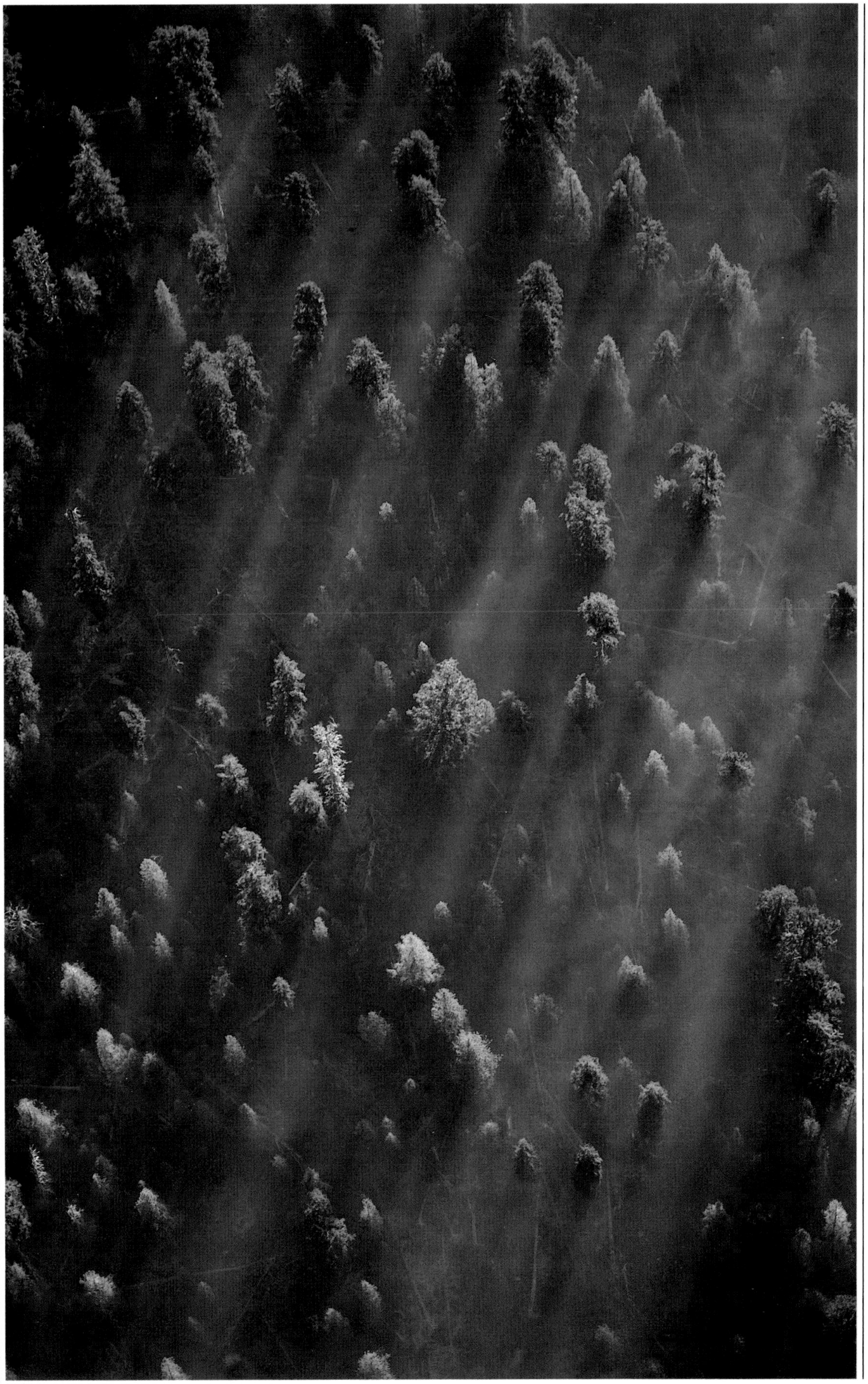

A stream of high-speed air arcing over the double crest
of Mount Shasta forms a lenticular cloud.

*Water boiling at 212 degrees Fahrenheit at Bumpass Hell on the
southern slopes of Lassen Volcanic National Park is evidence
of molten rock below the surface.*

*"Snow is falling on icy Shasta. Its rugged glaciers, steep lava-slopes,
and broad, swelling base are all gloriously snow-covered, and day
and night snow is still falling — snow on snow. The October storms
that began a month ago . . . fell with special emphasis upon the lofty
cone of Shasta, weaving and felting its lavish cross of snow-crystals,
fold over fold, and clothing the whole massive mountain in richest
winter white."* — John Muir Summering in the Sierra

*T*he Pit River flows
over a bed of
solidified lava in the
Modoc National Wildlife
Refuge at Alturas.

Crags of volcanic material, remnants of a molten past, barely pierce a thin blanket of snow clinging to the slopes of Mount Lassen.

Overleaf: The Painted Dunes on the northeastern edge of Lassen Volcanic National Park are tinted with the colors of their fiery origin.

93

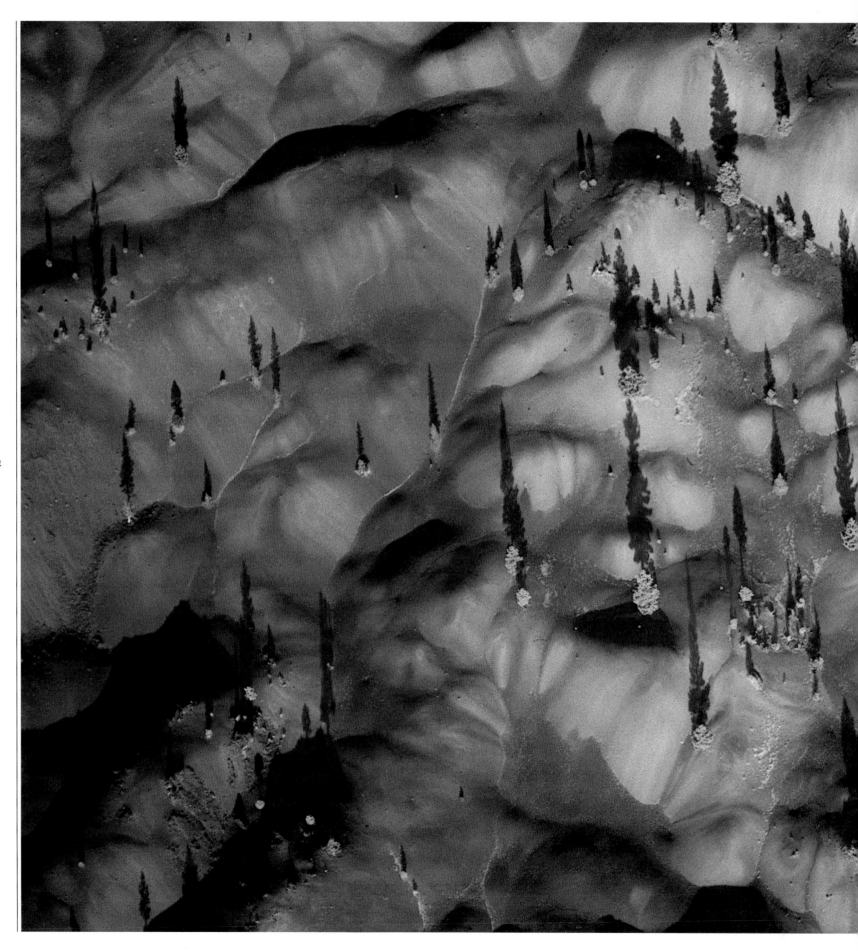

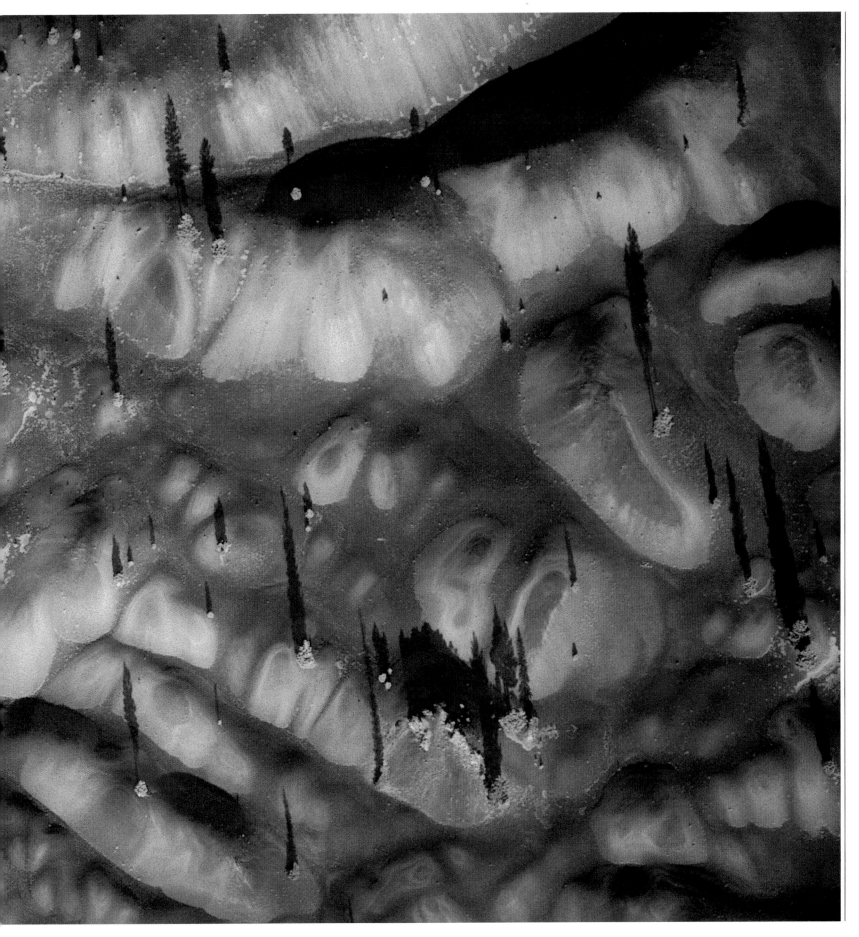

*T*he relentless return
of vegetation
is well advanced on the
flanks and interior of
Mount Hoffman.

Cinder Butte, on the outskirts of Lava Beds National Monument, remains denuded.

97

*P*onderosa pines dominate the fertile high ground
while sagebrush claims the low ground in
this area of Lava Beds National Monument.

Pelicans soar in ecstasy at Tule Lake National Wildlife Refuge.

" 'The Lava Beds' . . . are a portion of an ancient flood of dense black
lava, dipping north-eastward at a low angle. They are about as
destitute of soil as a glacial pavement, and though the surface is
generally level, it is dotted with hillocks and rough crater-like pits
and traversed in every direction by a net-work of yawning fissures,
forming a combination of topographical conditions of a very rare
and striking character." — *John Muir Summering in the Sierra*

Mojave and Colorado Deserts

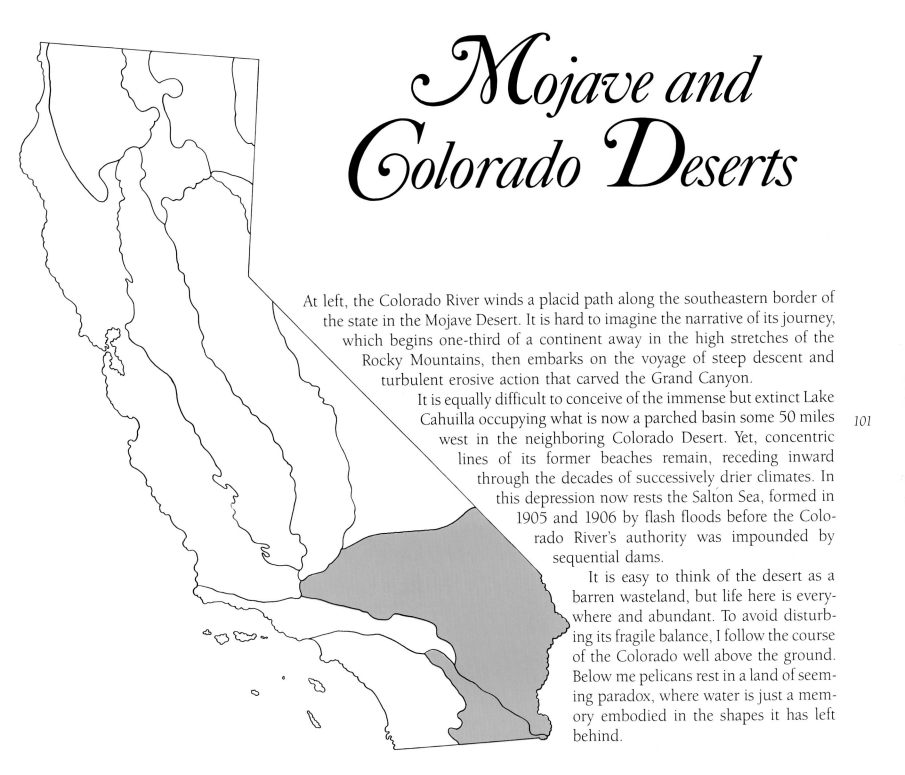

At left, the Colorado River winds a placid path along the southeastern border of the state in the Mojave Desert. It is hard to imagine the narrative of its journey, which begins one-third of a continent away in the high stretches of the Rocky Mountains, then embarks on the voyage of steep descent and turbulent erosive action that carved the Grand Canyon.

It is equally difficult to conceive of the immense but extinct Lake Cahuilla occupying what is now a parched basin some 50 miles west in the neighboring Colorado Desert. Yet, concentric lines of its former beaches remain, receding inward through the decades of successively drier climates. In this depression now rests the Salton Sea, formed in 1905 and 1906 by flash floods before the Colorado River's authority was impounded by sequential dams.

It is easy to think of the desert as a barren wasteland, but life here is everywhere and abundant. To avoid disturbing its fragile balance, I follow the course of the Colorado well above the ground. Below me pelicans rest in a land of seeming paradox, where water is just a memory embodied in the shapes it has left behind.

*The rugged badlands of the Palo Verde Mountains (left)
lie within a few miles of Colorado River waters (right),
yet the extremes of this scorched environment prevail.*

*Overleaf: In the Devils Playground near Kelso, fusible rock
once poured over the sands of time.*

"We tend to think of places like the Arctic, the Antarctic, the Gobi,
the Sahara, the Mojave, as primitive, but there are in fact no
primitive or even primeval landscapes. Neither are there permanent
landscapes. And nowhere is the land empty or underdeveloped. It
cannot be improved upon with technological assistance. The land, an
animal that contains all other animals, is vigorous and alive."

— Barry Lopez, *Arctic Dreams*

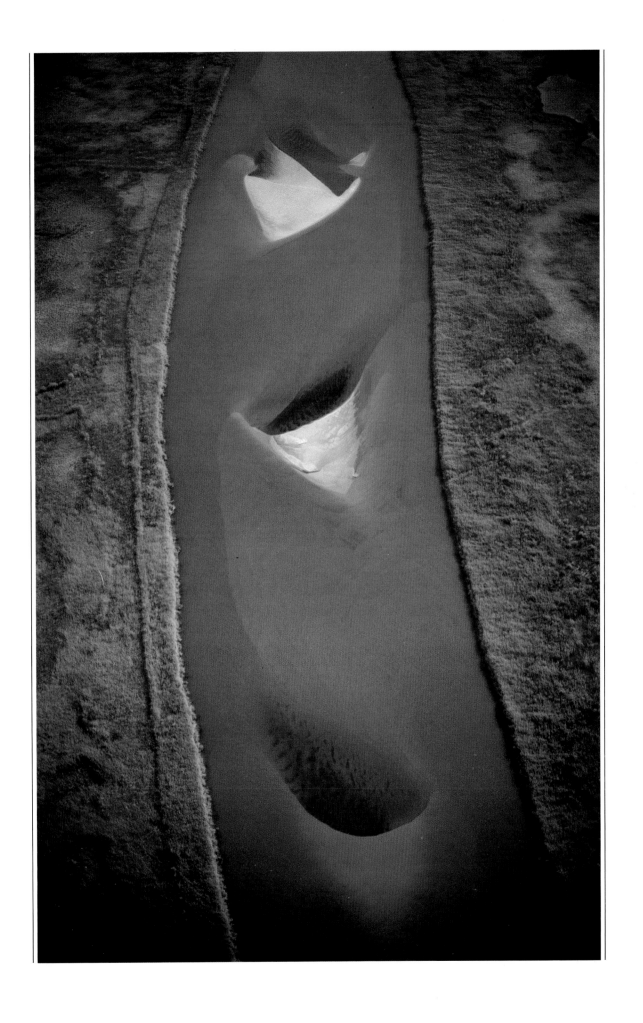

*The tamed waters of the Colorado River deposit
sand bars, providing a resting-place for
pelicans at the Imperial National Wildlife Refuge.*

*Lake Havasu, a man-made bulge in the Colorado River,
issues through a desiccated though bountiful land.*

"There are many areas in the desert where drinkable
water lies within a few feet of the surface, indicated by
the mesquite and the bunch grass. . . . It is this
nearness of unimagined help that makes the tragedy of
desert deaths." — Mary Austin, *The Land of Little Rain*

On the gentle rise of the Big Maria Mountains, ancestral Californians inscribed their likeness in dust.

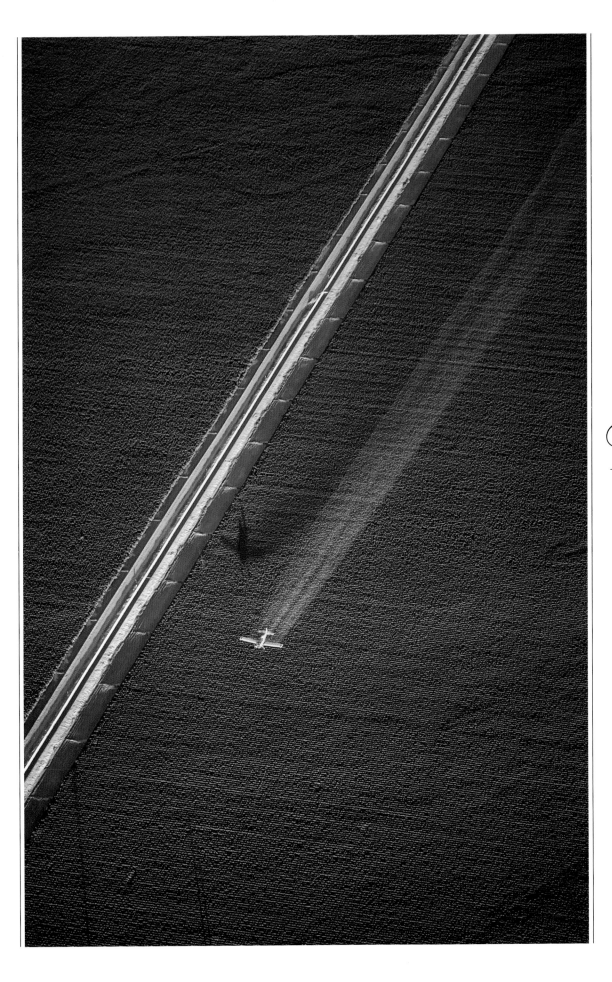

The marks we leave on the land today just a few miles away in Ripley are no less telling of our culture.

$\mathscr{A}$ll things to all people, the Colorado River is a source of
fresh water, a playground for the city-weary, the
lifeblood of precious ecological habitats and the squiggly
political boundary for the southeastern corner of the state.

The Algodones Dunes, the largest stretch of desert sands
in North America, catch fire at the break of day.

"Out West, the west of the mesas and the unpatented hills, there is
more sky than any place in the world. It does not sit flatly on the rim
of earth, but begins somewhere out in the space in which the earth is
poised, hollows more, and is full of clean winey winds. There are
some odors, too, that get into the blood. . . .

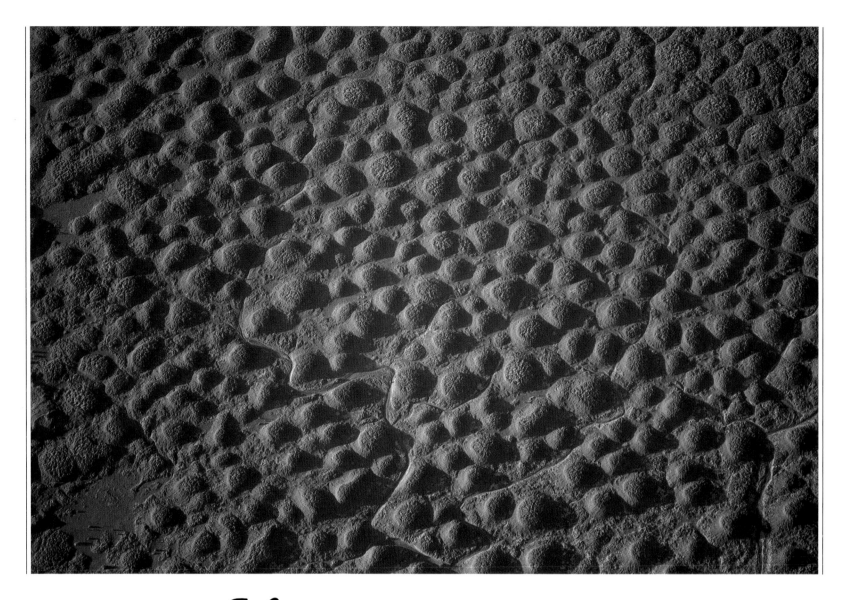

Natural patterns overtake the land at Danby Lake (left), while tractors harvest linear designs south of Blythe (right).

. . . *There is the spring smell of sage that is the warning that sap is beginning to work in a soil that looks to have none of the juices of life in it; it is the sort of smell that sets one thinking what a long furrow the plough would turn up here, the sort of smell that is the beginning of new leafage, is best at the plant's best, and leaves a pungent trail where wild cattle crop."*

— Mary Austin, *The Land of Little Rain*

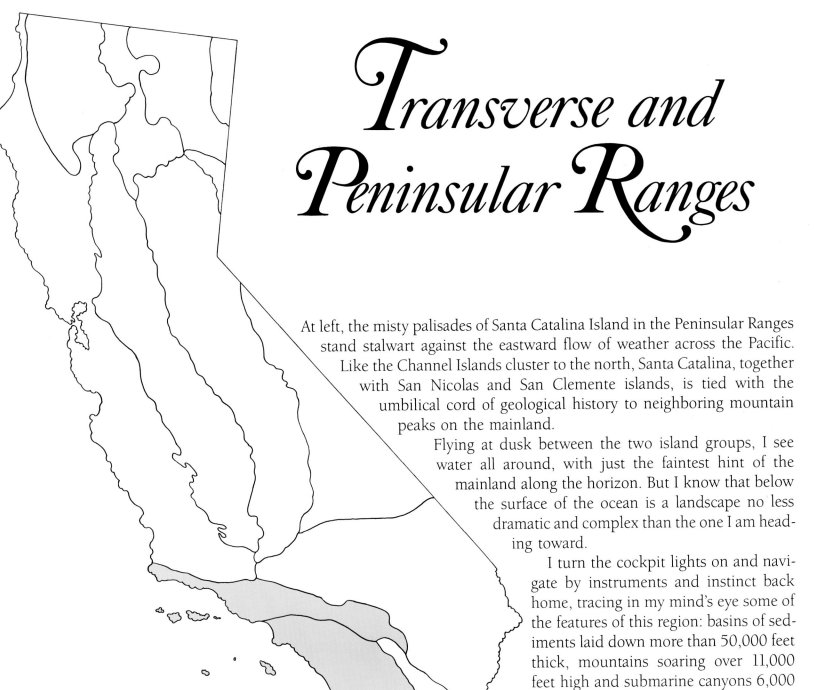

Transverse and Peninsular Ranges

At left, the misty palisades of Santa Catalina Island in the Peninsular Ranges stand stalwart against the eastward flow of weather across the Pacific. Like the Channel Islands cluster to the north, Santa Catalina, together with San Nicolas and San Clemente islands, is tied with the umbilical cord of geological history to neighboring mountain peaks on the mainland.

Flying at dusk between the two island groups, I see water all around, with just the faintest hint of the mainland along the horizon. But I know that below the surface of the ocean is a landscape no less dramatic and complex than the one I am heading toward.

I turn the cockpit lights on and navigate by instruments and instinct back home, tracing in my mind's eye some of the features of this region: basins of sediments laid down more than 50,000 feet thick, mountains soaring over 11,000 feet high and submarine canyons 6,000 feet deep.

Overleaf: *The loftiest peak south of the Sierra Nevada, Mount San Gorgonio glows pink and orange in the summer twilight.*

117

*Neither rock nor vegetation can take hold on the steep
avalanche chutes of Mount San Antonio,
also known as Old Baldy.*

*With the San Jacinto Mountains as a backdrop, shadows
cast by piles of granite boulders stream across the dry plateau
of Joshua Tree National Monument.*

"Between the desert and the sea a narrow belt of
valley, hill, and mountain of wonderful beauty is
found. Over this coastal zone there falls a balm
distilled from the great ocean, as gentle showers and
refreshing dews bathe the land. . . .

*A rainbow falls from a rare thundershower along the edge
of the Salton Sea, Anza-Borrego Desert State Park.*

*The winds of time have weathered these southern slopes of
Santa Cruz Island, Channel Islands National Park, into arms
that seem to reach toward their kin in the Santa Monica Mountains.*

*. . . When rains come the emerald hills laugh with delight as
bourgeoning bloom is spread in the sunlight. When the rains have
ceased all the verdure turns to gold. Then slowly the hills are
brinded until the rains come again, when verdure and bloom again
peer through the tawny wreck of the last year's greenery."*
— John Wesley Powell, *The Exploration of the Colorado River and its Canyons*

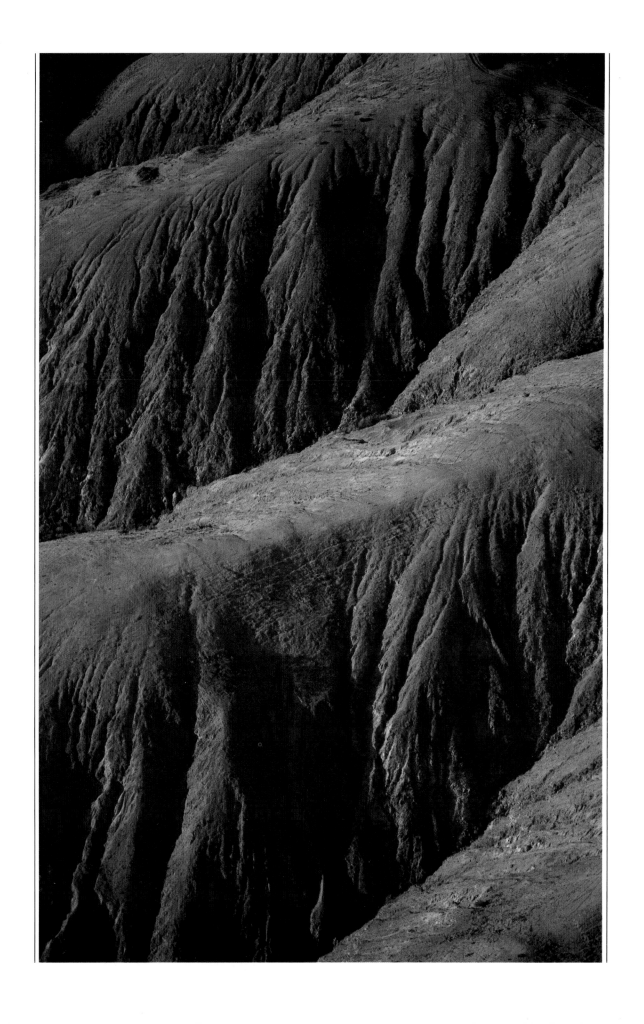

A snowy San Jacinto
Mountain
*casts evening shadows
across the thirsty
Coachella Valley.*

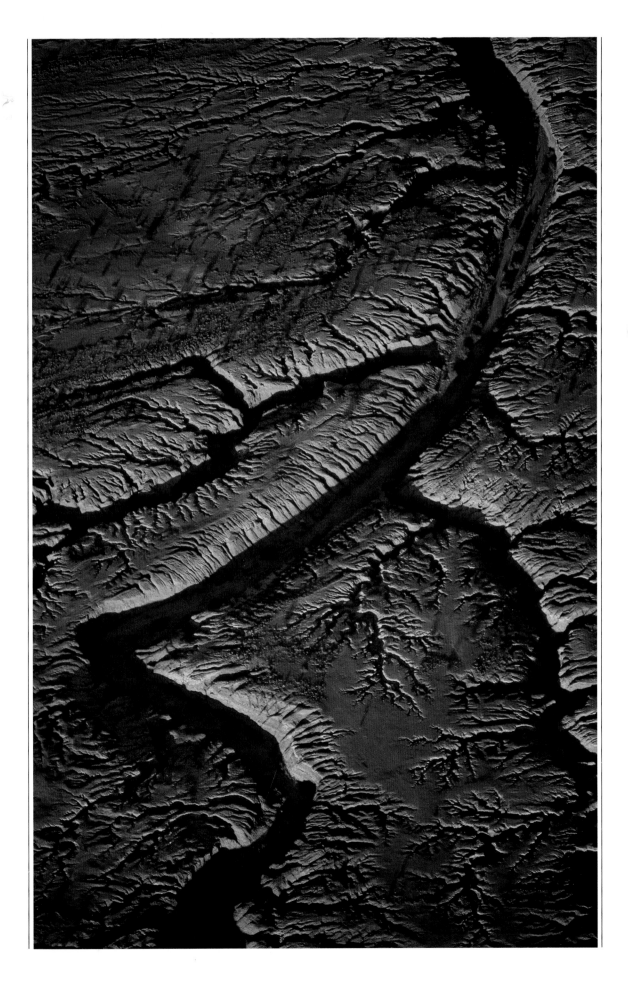

*O*ver millions of years, intermittent rains have etched treelike dendritic drainage patterns in the thick sedimentary layers of Anza-Borrego Desert State Park.

Overleaf: *Like the hidden segment of an iceberg, the vertical flanks of Santa Catalina Island extend more than one mile below the ocean waves.*

123

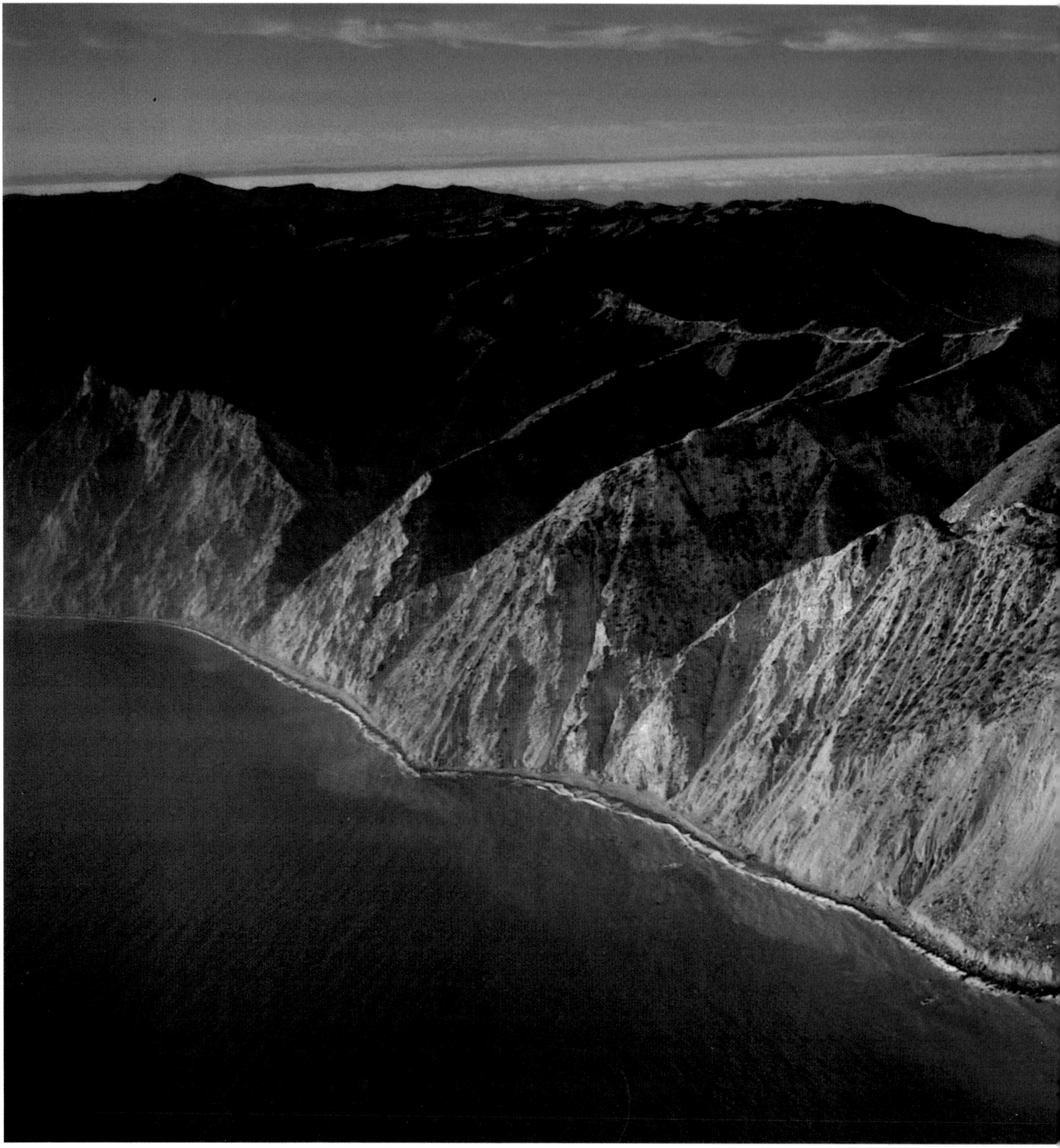

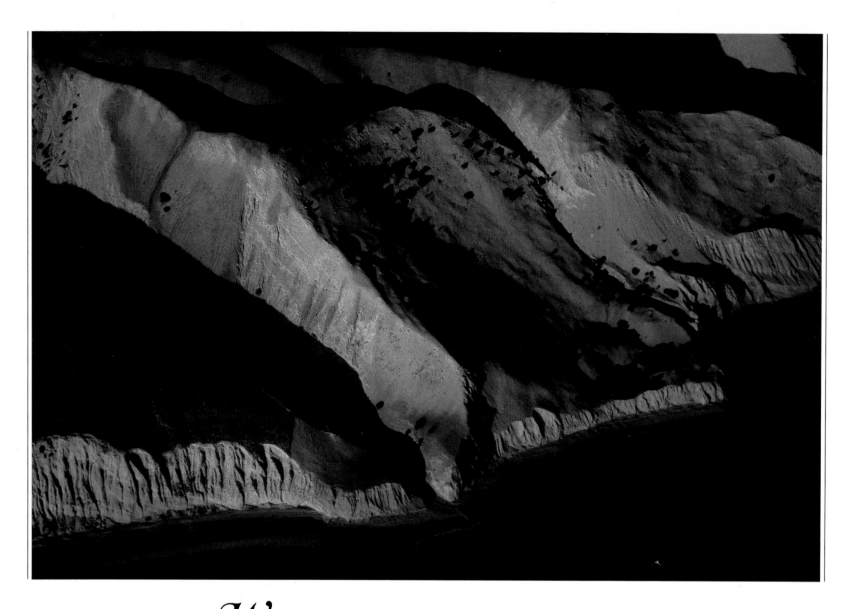

*W*ith steep cliffs, gigantic sea caves, sandy beaches and
protected tide pools, the varied topography
of Santa Cruz Island supports a remarkable array
of flora and fauna.

The ingredients are the same — trees, rocks and snow — but
the effects are polar opposites, with San Jacinto Mountain (top)
radiating the warm tones of the setting sun, and Hot Springs
Mountain (bottom) displaying the icy blue of early morning.

*"Whatever evaluation we finally make of a stretch of land, however,
no matter how profound or accurate, we will find it inadequate. The
land retains an identity of its own, still deeper and more subtle than
we can know."* — Barry Lopez, *Arctic Dreams*

TECHNICAL INFORMATION

The photographs in this book were produced on 35mm equipment, with lenses ranging from 28mm up to 300mm. No filters were used other than a skylight and occasionally a polarizer. The camera was hand-held and pointed through the open window of the aircraft. Shutter speeds were maximized in most cases, but dipped down to 1/15 of a second for some low-light situations.

While out on photographic missions, Barrie Rokeach acted also as the pilot, flying single-engine high-wing aircraft (he is a commercially rated instrument pilot with more than 20 years' flying experience). Altitudes extended from 1,000 feet up to 17,950 feet above sea level.

Acknowledgements

This book would not have been possible without the love and support of my family. To my parents for their guidance and enthusiasm, to Sharron and Don for their warmth and encouragement, and to my wife, Brenda, for her companionship and inspiration, I am deeply grateful.   — B.R.

A harsh bay on San Miguel Island, the westernmost of the Channel Islands, is polished to a chrome finish by Pacific winds.